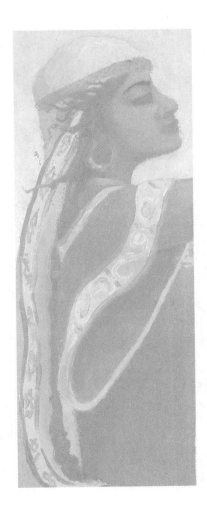

A Telling Place

Reflections on stories of women in the Bible

Joy Mead

WILD GOOSE PUBLICATIONS

Copyright © 2002 Joy Mead
First published 2002 by
Wild Goose Publications, Fourth Floor, Savoy House,
140 Sauchiehall Street, Glasgow G2 3DH, UK,
the publishing division of the Iona Community.
Scottish Charity No. SCO03794.
Limited Company Reg. No. SCO96243.

ISBN 1 901557 68 5

Cover painting © 2002 Mrdula Basi
Cover design © 2002 Wild Goose Publications

A catalogue record for this book is available from the British Library.

Overseas distribution:
N. America: Novalis Publishing & Distribution, 49 Front St. E., Toronto, Canada M5E 1B3
Australia: Willow Connection Pty Ltd, Unit 4A, 3-9 Kenneth Road, Manly Vale, NSW 2093
New Zealand: Pleroma Christian Supplies, Higginson St., Otane 4170, Central Hawkes Bay

Permission to reproduce any part of this work in Australia
or New Zealand should be sought from Willow Connection.

Printed by Bell & Bain, Thornliebank, Glasgow, UK

Contents

Women of the New Testament: followers, messengers, lovers, friends

Foreword

It is a privilege to write a few words about this book, which I have watched taking shape. It is a unique piece of work by a quietly remarkable woman. Joy and I have a long friendship sustained by bread and words: shared meals, telephone conversations, family letters about birth and death and down-to-earth, often funny, situations; poems in the post, carefully penned or speeding through cyberspace.

As women who grew up in the second half of the 20th century, we share experiences of a changing world – of family relationships through which we grow and are enriched, by which we are sometimes defined or constrained; of education which can pigeonhole or liberate; of living through a time when women have found a voice and a vocabulary, while men have struggled to do the same for their experience.

Becoming members of the Iona Community means being part of a movement within the Churches, a commitment to peace and justice, to rebuilding community in the different places where members of this dispersed community live and work and worship, and, in the words of one of the community's prayers, to find 'new ways … to touch the hearts of all'.

Poetry creates 'a touching place' (which is the name of one of the many new hymns from the Iona Community), and the title of this book is a play on that phrase. Joy has looked at the Bible as a sequence of stories, and has imagined the women who appear from time to time in its pages telling their own stories, rather than turning up briefly on the margins of a narrative which reflects a world perceived and a society led by men. As she imagines their experience, and their perspective, she is also expressing her belief that this is not just about 'women's issues', but is relevant to both men and women. As she says, 'Women's stories and their telling reveal the interrelatedness at the heart of life.'

Some of these poems speak to me more powerfully than others. I have been refreshed by 'Living Water' for years, since it first appeared in the magazine I edited. I am still unsure about 'Miriam's Song', might have written differently myself about Mary and Martha and continue, each time I listen to the world news, to remember and be deeply moved by 'Sisera's Mother', which only Joy could have written. Reading this collection I made a delighted discovery of 'Apple Life'. Women are different, and my friend Joy doesn't always speak for me or every other woman – but her poetry opens doors to dialogue between women and men, makes telling points and vivid, valuable connections.

It is an expression of her belief, which as a fellow human being and person of faith I share, that everything in God's world is connected.

Jan Sutch Pickard
Warden, Iona Community

Women at the Well

Thirsty people, wanting
containers for their needs
and their longings;
women with the means
to draw fresh water;
colour, activity
fertile wetness,
bodies of hope –
gather around a possibility
of blossoming deserts
and flourishing people;
growing food
and healthy children.

A well is a telling place
where perceptions are changed
and tomorrow welcomed;
where hidden stories
bubble up joyfully
to heal and enliven
every part
of our shared being.

Introduction

There is a story in John's Gospel of an encounter between Jesus and a Samaritan woman at Jacob's Well. She gives him a drink; he talks with her. It is a sensitive story of meeting, giving and receiving – a telling place. But most of all it is a story of letting go all that seems to be most precious so that we might be free to become fully human. The woman leaves her water jar at the well and carries within herself the flowing water of life and hope. Flowing water, symbol of fertility, creativity and purity, is a questioning element. There is nothing certain, fixed or rigid about it.

The story of this meeting is one of the most poignant, holding together many stories told around the fluidity of water: Rachel's meeting with the angel-tracker Jacob at the same well, Pharaoh's daughter and the stream of life, Miriam beside the Red Sea … All sorts of things happen around water: creative, celebratory, promising things.

Jesus has no jar; the woman puts down her jar. Something free and uncontained happens between two people at the well. There is a mutuality unprecedented in New Testament times. The water flows and the people are free to grow and be.

When I was on Iona recently a woman, also staying at the Abbey, approached me and asked my full name. Until that moment she'd known me only as 'Joy'. Then she told me that a copy of one of my poems was given to her some years ago at a retreat and she'd kept it pinned on her mirror ever since. She read it every day and it had helped her through a difficult time. I was moved by this. The poem concerned, 'Living Water', has become the basis for this book about women at the margins; women who are in someone else's story but seek their own; women without names, or with forgotten names; women with telling ways who in love and silence ponder, listen and give. It's also about being overwhelmed by joy or sorrow, about insights and questions, often wordless, carried on the body, flowing through the silent part of our being. It's about looking into the puzzling heart of all things – like Jesus and the Samaritan woman, or Jacob and Rachel, at the well. They have always been there: informal networks of women around a 'well'; women connecting with other women across family boundaries in ways that make differences in whole communities as well as in the lives of families. Sometimes their presence is more significant than others, perhaps nowhere more so than in the story of Ruth (see p 56).

I am attempting to understand the significance to community experience of an individual inner feeling (not letting anyone tell me the personal isn't political!) and to value images and forms of thinking that might begin in the home but need, perhaps, to be extended beyond the home to challenge and become integrated with traditional political thinking. Women's work – food and drink given to strangers and friends out of our own resources, loving unpaid work that carers do (underrated in Bible times, underrated today) is explored and valued. I have tried to tell of what happens when the experience of the margins and the women's stories – not believed through the ages ('They, with the other women, told these things to the apostles. But the story appeared to them to be nonsense …' Luke 24:10) – become central. I hope this is a bit more than the old feminist reading of the other side of the story, for it seeks to be about alternative ways of thinking, being and seeing. We see how emblematic the stories of these Bible women are – how intimately our own.

A Telling Place is a whole story – so I have started with the Hebrew Bible and worked through to the New Testament. Like the Children of Israel generally, the women of the Hebrew Bible are finding their way, finding their story. Many are in the shadows, the silent part of another story. Then in the New Testament they become disciples, followers, lovers, friends. There are many stories of women from whom Jesus learns.

Much of the Bible probably never actually happened but is people's way, through poetry and story, of trying to understand how things are for them as individuals and communities. Memory and imagination do not work chronologically. So I have not necessarily arranged the stories chronologically but in a way that contributes to the whole story, the wholeness, of this book. The stories are about how people live and see their living, how they interpret, express and connect. Rachel links with the Samaritan woman who met Jesus at the same well, Hannah's and Mary's songs are much the same, while widows are central to the prophetic visions of Elijah and Jesus.

So there is no beginning to begin at and there will be no conclusion, for this is not a book of certainties and answers but of explorations and questions – questions that challenge the fallacy of no alternative. Any message will be carried on the body like Mary's song, like the living water. There will be no frantic search for Meaning, Truth or Purpose … but looking, living, paying attention, being sensitive to the layers of life … discovering what it is to be human … to be alive.

Joy Mead
Great Missenden, 2002

Faith Mother

I feel your nearness more acutely now
old woman: the last to be freed
from cruel joke and mocking cliché.

No longer put to death as witch
but often confined as confused.
Your seeing is threatening,

(At menopause they say
women often see the devil.)

and stands in the way
of conformity to a pattern
in which the human body is beautiful
only if it is young, shapely
and smells good.

But like Sarah long ago
you can still laugh
at the overlarge egos
of old men
hungry for lost dreams.

Your inner beauty
is the mysterious wisdom
of a heart, as yet, unbowed.

Your long and earthy memory
holds the experience of ages
of seeing and being
of waiting and pondering
all things in your heart.

Your ancient understanding
could even now be our hope
and our salvation.

Women of the Hebrew Bible

Finding her story

Finding Her Story

We might sensibly begin with Eve but there's someone else who never made the Christian or Jewish canons and she's in us all. I love the story of Lilith (see pp 24–27), particularly if she is seen as a dybbuk of delight. A dybbuk, in Jewish folklore, is a restless soul compelled to take possession of a living person and speak through him or her. Michelene Wandor in her poem 'Lilith's Dance' describes her like this:

I am the dybbuk of delight
I slip into the souls
of those who need me

perhaps you breathed
just a little
too much life, a sniffle too long
but once tasting the air
I would not be still, not
be silent, not return
to my feet of clay

and so makes Lilith a creative muse who speaks through women in a voice we might not always recognise but can't deny.

In the Beginning ...

Lilith is the first woman to appear in Jewish myth and story. She is formed from the earth, equal in all ways to the first man, Adam, and she resists his claims to superiority. Male scholars and rabbis have obscured or overlaid the story of Lilith. Often they have made her a malevolent spirit and sexual harridan. In one telling of the story, she is banished to the wilderness. Her name cannot be found in the Torah, the central canon of Jewish scripture, but is in the Talmud and other more esoteric writings like the Zohar, a Kabbalistic work of the thirteenth century.

Adam, Lilith and Eve

Lilith, Adam's first
his equal
amazed
at any suggestion
of difference.

Adam wants relationship
with God,
exclusive, guarded –
and seeks to interpret
God's will to her

But that is not
the way. She has mind
just like him
and irrepressible spirit.

So she ups and leaves
Adam and his God.

Then comes Eve –
– chattel –
suppressing the outsider,
the wild woman,
all that is feared
by good wives.

Lilith doesn't abandon Eve
in the garden.
She stretches out a hand
of friendship and freedom
so that together,
creative free spirit
and mother of all life,
they are ready
to look death
in the face.

The story of Eve and Lilith together is a hopeful sequel to centuries of malign male commentary on them both.

Lilith and Eve

Adam and Lilith are created equal but Adam soon seeks the dominant role and Lilith objects. She will not lie beneath him when they make love! Eventually she flies away and Adam complains to God (in a voice I think we'll recognise!) '….. that uppity woman you sent me has gone and deserted me.' God tries to persuade Lilith to return (familiar?) and when she won't he creates, this time from within Adam himself, another companion: Eve.

Adam and Eve have a satisfactory relationship although Eve feels constrained and her sense of self is underdeveloped. Her gifts go unrecognised and unrewarded. Adam does important work and has this exclusive relationship with God which she begins to resent.

Lilith, alone now, tries to return to the Garden and once Eve catches a glimpse of her which sows seeds of curiosity within her. She begins to think about the limitations of her own life.

One day, walking in the Garden, Eve sees a young apple tree which she and Adam had planted. One of its branches now stretches over the garden wall. She climbs it and swings over the wall.

Lilith is waiting on the other side. They talk. They share stories. They teach each other many things. Back in the Garden, Adam talks with God. Both are confused. Something has failed to go according to plan. 'I am who I am,' thinks God, 'but must become who I will become.'

God and Adam are expectant and afraid the day Eve, mother of all living things, and Lilith return to the Garden bursting with possibilities, ready to rebuild it together.

All about Eve

What Eliza Sharples wrote in 1872 about the fallacy of the Fall is relevant now:

'If that was a fall, sirs, it was a glorious fall and such a fall as is now wanted …'

Eve's is a good story of struggle, maturity and hope. For knowledge of death is also knowledge of life. Deeper understanding brings with it big questions, the awareness of the possibility of transformation, the passion to make and make again, a care for humble things which might lead to such ordinary miracles as rebuilding lives, planting trees or turning derelict city space into gardens and places for children to play.

Eve in a Community Garden

Adaptable as dandelions
undefeated by broken streets,
and city waste-lands,
today's Eves come in jeans and tee-shirts,
looking for a wall-less room
of their own
encouraged by dreams of
beans as green
as last summer's love,
carrots, cucumbers
and creamy new potatoes,
courgettes and currants,
sweet yellow peppers,
plums of royal purple
soft on the tongue,
armfuls of sunflowers

Beneath an apple tree
long retired – recovered soil
is rich with unexpected seeds
tough enough to challenge conformity
and celebrate a random paradise:
a scarlet outburst
of poppies, appropriate tribute
to our long ago sister
who saw the apple and knew
that it was beautiful.

Apple Life

She wants to bite
this small globe,
the unforgettable apple –
holds colours
of an autumn hillside;
the sunlight glow
of long summer days;
an earthy ripeness;
a tongue-tingling sharp sweetness,
luscious wetness and cool crispness
– the taste of Eden.
Just one bite explodes in her mouth.
Is it too much to want
knowledge and the garden,
sweetness and ashes?
She sees the fruit fall,
and rot,
the ripe seed die
in the ground
so that tomorrow
the air may be filled
with the heady scent
of apple blossom.

Knowledge –
of what exactly?

There is, it seems, appropriate response
to a naked woman offering fruit
and promising understanding.

Don't say, 'Well done. Now people
are grown up and may live wholly
and look death
in the face.'

No. History it seems
begins with needlework:
the need to make and sew
garments to cover adequately
worrying bits of the human body.

Sin on the other hand
isn't happening in the garden
but out in the nowhere place
where Cain kills Abel.

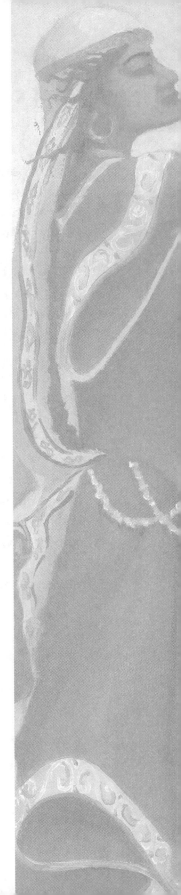

Out of the Shadows of His Story:
the questions … and the hope

The stories of Eve, mother of all living things, giving birth and nurture, and Lilith, creative free spirit refusing to be confined or controlled, give us images of womanhood and the search for wholeness and self. The Hebrew Bible tells of many seekers and searchers: struggling against oppressors; knowing their own longing; reaching out or reaching back with knowledge, insight and longing; looking for a language to express the inexpressible; bearing the inexpressible on their bodies; releasing strong feelings in laughter.

What of the women selected as heroines by patriarchal standards: Jael, Deborah, Judith? … What questions do their stories raise? What is this honour? Is it the same honour to which Jephthah's nameless daughter and the nameless woman in Judges 19 were sacrificed? Then there are women who wordlessly and prophetically wait and watch (Sisera's Mother), question and challenge (Shiphrah and Puah), serve and give (Rachel).

Many of the stories have dark sides. If we give them our full attention big questions arise. We are led to explore lost knowledges, experiences that died with the women, where written material is scarce and we can only begin to imagine. But unless we reclaim the stories by looking at moments of being, remembering and relating and ask difficult questions, the possibility of another way will never be contemplated and there will be no healing.

Rachel weeps for all the generations, and the long line of women beside a river of tears begin to recognise the hope in Miriam and join her dance of joy.

Woman Without a Name

Judges 19

Woman
without a name,
raped and abused
until break of day
then taken limb by limb
through the length of the land.
What symbolism is this?
What do I hear
in your silences?

Who questions your abuse
and the crime
against female sexuality,
when the only question is misuse
of man's property?

Can I stand in solidarity
with your pain
and let the silence be
wordless?

Is your silence
louder than the cry
from the cross?

Lot's Wife

(for all exiles and asylum seekers)
Genesis 19:26

How many salt tears
to cleanse the dirt
from a burning, gaping wound;
to begin a healing process
or an escape from blandness?

Salt in the wind,
the sea in our blood.

Take to the sea;
take to the desert;
or some other source
of fear.
Lick the salt for life
in the over-savoured wasteland.
Carry the salt
to a saltless land,
savouring past loves
in a new place of tears.

Salt in the wind
the sea in our blood.

Crystallising in one backward glance
old knowledges, ancient understandings,
you become in the turning
the shape and piquancy
of the many salt tears
you weep for home.

Sarah's Circle

Genesis 18:12; Genesis 28:12

You laughed long ago, old Sarah;
the laughter of all living things
which expresses ecstasy and sensuality;
gentleness and nurture;
earthiness and openness;
laughter which allows no distance
between us and God
but makes a never-ending circle
of compassion
out of a curve
of sorrowing hands;
for your laughter is fruitfulness;
your laughter is creation;
your laughter is the celebrating,
earth-orientated dance
of interdependence
which turns its back on Jacob's Ladder
to make a ring of joy
that takes the spirit
round and round, not up and down;
takes the spirit round and round
but always out and out
to all whose earthy hands
are open wide.

Songlines for Sarah and Hagar

Genesis 18:12; Genesis 21:15

From the immense shadows
the sound of a desperate cry
cuts across Sarah's laughter
and the dance on the green.

The sound of suffering is shaped
to the song of the earth
and the way of the people's dreams;
while the search is still
for priests and altars
and words that will not betray.

But the priests are all unfrocked
and the altars somewhere else.
Only the earth's echoing wail
sings the way of hope
along untrodden paths
where inspiration and lost wisdom
may be recovered.
For hope has no path
and is wordless;
hope is not mine to bring
but to recognise in the sharing
of bread with Hagar
who suffers, and hopes, and waits
at the margins.

Rachel

Genesis 29–35

Some way from the angels
of Bethel, Ben-oni's longed-for birth
takes Rachel's breath away.
Bargaining for mandrakes,
concealing household gods
uneasy dreaming
all move into
emptiness.

A silent memory
holds true –
Rachel becomes her Self:
all breath, pure colour;
dappled, brindled, spotted:
angel-light of our imaginings:
shaped in sheep and goats
 – named for the angel-tracker
Jacob's love
of his dark and beautiful bride;
 – woven for ever
into the multi-coloured story
of Joseph's unforgettable coat.

Rachel's Tears

Jeremiah 31:15

Look into the faces
of the sorrowing children.
They will break your heart.

Rachel weeps for her children
and for generations
as yet unborn.

Woman without comfort or consolation,
she keeps a timeless vigil
for nameless mothers
and their missing sons and daughters;
for all who pick up the pieces,
collect the wounded,
bring home the dead,
and wait for the bread
to feed the living.

Death does not dry her tears.
They wash over history
 – into the places
words will never reach.

Look into the faces
of the sorrowing children.
They will break your heart.

Scarlet Women

Red ribbons or cords –
bookmarks in the pages
of history;
writing in the margins
 – surprise or warning.
They alert me to interruptions
in a genealogy.

Now I see
women's hands reach out;
tears stain the pages;
I hear cries echoing
from a far place.

I begin to wonder
about the missing stories.
What would they tell
these free and generous beings
who are all things to all men?

Tamar and Rahab –
prostituted for a storyteller's pleasure
manipulated to show the hand
 of history
manhandled to proclaim
the greatness of Israel's God
and his guidance
at their cost
at all cost.

Tamar, we are told in Genesis 38, pretends to be a prostitute; Rahab, who features in Joshua 2, is a prostitute. Neither tells her own story nor is it told by another. The storyteller uses them, takes his pleasure of both and when they are no longer needed (for theological purposes) he discards them and we hear no more until surprisingly they reappear in the genealogy of Jesus in the first chapter of Matthew's Gospel.

Dinah

Genesis 34

'Is our sister to be treated as a whore?'
– unreachable words buzz in her ears
as she sits apart
in a place of pondering
– a woman's place.

'Is our sister to be treated as a whore?'
– makes heroes in a story;
plays to male pride
but bigger questions
loom in the heart
of the woman watching
as men, using her name,
plunder a town,
slaughter men, slay flocks,
carry off wealth,
women and children.

'Is our sister to be treated as a whore?'
– is a battle cry; a flag to wave;
a symbol, badge, sign or emblem
to endorse violence
and gratify an unnamed instinct
unrelated to the wholly human desires
of a woman who has no rights,
no possessions … no voice …

and so no country
or town … or place …
or body to call her own.

'Is our sister to be treated as a whore?'
 – hollow words now.
As the sun goes down
on aggression and hatred,
rioting and violence
there are different questions:

'Who asked the women?'
 and
'What now is honour?'

Shiphrah and Puah

Exodus 1

There is always the possibility
of another way;

always the possibility
of changing theology, thinking,
conditioning

always the possibility
of taking co-operation
seriously;

of sharing food,
knowing there will be enough
to go round.

There is always the possibility
of rejecting violence – totally;
of not buying the war game, the toy gun …;

always the possibility that one day
plastic models in cornflakes packets
will not be destroyers
but peacemakers.

There is always the possibility
of responding creatively:
trusting vulnerability … smallness,
gentleness … tiny signs
of new life.

There is always the possibility
of not obeying orders;
of being midwives
at the risky birth
of hope.

The story of the discovery of Moses in the bulrushes is a telling image of relinquishing control and letting go; not claiming the abundance for ourselves only but giving it back to the stream of life.

Pharaoh's Daughter

Exodus 2:10

They are everywhere:
small Hebrew children,
lifeblood of a people,
fertile, fecund, flowing:
a river of life
she walks beside.

The basket: a floating flower,
comes towards her on the stream
offering its contents
like a promise.

Her hands reach out
disturbing the glistening flow.
Broody birds rise,
their wings beating wildly
like her startled heart
as she draws the baby
from the water.

Then the girl, her eyes alert
from minding, moves
to her side, whispering
of mother's milk

while she, childless
daughter of Pharaoh,
longs to feed honey
to another woman's child.

The wind off the water
caresses her urgency
with the coolness
of time that is always early
and will neither allow her to pass by
nor let her claim this abundance
as if it were her own.

She gives him back
to the stream of life;
to be nourished
in the knowledge and resilience
he will need, to survive
and lead his people
to freedom.

Jael and Deborah

Judges 4 and 5

A woman drives a nail
through the head of a sleeping man.
Bones crack, flesh tears, blood runs.
She stakes him to the ground
and a life of good and evil,
like most others,
pours out into the waiting earth.
This, the story tells,
saves a nation.

When she sees another woman dancing
and hears the victory song,
does her body remember
the blood on its hands?

When the judgement for the future
is a time of lasting peace,
does she raise her voice
with the others in a song
of common joy
or is the only sound
her lonely weeping
for fragile humanity?

And if the women's triumph song
drowns the sound of quiet weeping
who will then say
there has to be
another way?

Abigail

(For Jan)

1 Samuel 25

'A blessing on your good sense'
peacemaker; affirming and lifegiving.
You see generously,
make an ordinary miracle
as lovely as a common flower
that blooms in a war zone
and fills the air
with the sweet scent
of human hope.

Michal

2 Samuel, 6:16–20; 2 Samuel 3:13–14

A man makes carnival
in a courtyard;
displays to captive eyes
a body all his own;
dances with abandon into
his story.

Above, immobile and secretive
a childless woman
watches and waits.
The window frames
her body long misused
as condition for negotiation
and deal; passed
around for pleasure,
not her own.

We see her set above us
in light and shadows – coloured –
like a Chagall window,
telling silently of suffering
and joy; showing us all life,
coming from everywhere
to this threshold place.
She outbursts
the frame described
to hold her.

The rhythm of her heartbeat
echoes beyond the indoor world
of her time and place.
She unites
home and street,
body and spirit
Her image, at the in-between place,
tells her story.

Sisera's Mother

Judges 5

Who does not cast a glance
to where an unnamed mother sits
silently, at the edge of her story?

Pondering in her heart
the things of his growing, she waits,
powerless and voiceless,
for the hoofbeat of his horses
on the soil of home;
while talk is of damsels
and dyed stuff
to grace a victor's neck;

She watches the dawning:
the gradual revealing
of a vast emptiness,
for many share the dying
but few the knowing.

The rays of the morning sun
pierce her heart
and her still body is the shape
of a multitude of grieving women;
for no one asks the mothers
when the talk is of war
and the spoils of war.

Judith

The Apocrypha

Delightful ambiguity – woman of prayer
and property; we see you wise
in the ways of the human heart.
We see you grasp the workings
of the minds of men massed
in force; caught in the grip
of a heartless logic.
They neither fathom
the maker of mortal beings,
nor know the Lord
who stamps out wars.

Woman of beauty and hidden resources,
you are love, law and the struggle
for life.

Moses said, 'Choose Life.'
You, self-defining woman,
see a side of truth
often concealed;
look to a forgotten
promised land
somewhere;

not a land so much
as space for all
to live in;
not forgotten so much
as half-remembered –
a milk and honey place
of living, laughter and love-of-life
beckoning from the future;
never purely good
nor irredeemably evil,
holy
in this world.

Jephthah's Daughter

(For all abused women)

Judges 11:35

We go, Sisters of Israel, year by year
to reconnect with the broken roots
of our being; and remember
Jephthah's daughter.

In the desert places,
we become
a theatre of women:

dancing for the spirit
that haunts our ageing minds
with memories not our own;

dancing for the fragility
and tenderness
of all living things;

dancing to an unnamed woman's
unwritten tune.

Four days we mourn,
in a story re-created,
in a metaphor lived,
the threshold moment
when she steps out
from innocence …
to death.

For nobody tells her
that the song she sings
is her own.

One man says: '… such calamity
you have brought upon me …'

One man does not hear the voice
of God in the song of youth;

One man does not see the shape of God
in a dancing female form.

One man does not know how to celebrate
the frail, the small, the fragile.

And her front door
is my front door.

Two stories stand out from all the others in the Hebrew Bible: Ruth, a story of stories, a story of hunger … and Esther, a story of words and laughter, a story of feasting. They are complete books carrying women's names and experience and, unlike many of the earlier stories of women in the Bible, they tell of women working together, of women's companionship and solidarity, of their undying hope.

Ruth ... and Right Relationship

The story of Ruth is a literary gem, a brief moment of peace in a troubled world. It is probably the most authentic female voice in the Hebrew Bible, and is a story about stories – about sharing our own experience – and about relationship.

It is a tale told intimately through the use of dialogue – unusual in Bible stories – through the use of oral wordplay, repetition of key words and alliteration, all of which stir our imagination. Feminine language brings the margins to the centre. There are no military or martial words; there is no direct theology. Everything is developed through experience and insight. Greetings and meetings are often and gentle. Encounters, relationships, care and compassion are what matter. The pattern of all life is here: community and isolation, famine and plenty, life and death, male and female. We see all aspects of women's lives from loss and invisibility right through to fulfilment and empowerment and visibility.

Ruth, the Moabite, is so converted and assimilated into Israelite culture that we might forget her origins. There is a big question: is there some incontrovertible essence that determines what it is to be Israeli, Palestinian, Moabite … a woman, or are these conditioned, constructed? Orpah's is the Moabite story. She returns to her mother's house (unusually in Bible stories as a whole, home in this story is defined by the mother), goes out of this story and so resonates with indigenous women often completely left out of history. She is the one who will carry on the sacred traditions of her own people. Such stories as hers are vital to enable silenced people to find a voice.

More ambivalence, other questions exist around the origins of Ruth's name, so significant to her Book. Traditionally, it has been seen as an abbreviation of *Re'uth*, or female companion. But some Bible scholars feel the name is from *rwh*, 'to water to saturation', which has special significance for this book and the women at the well.

And always in the background is a chorus of women. They have always been there and still are. Ruth is a useful source of information on and inspiration for informal associations of women – the personal is political when the interests of individual families are seen reflected in the collective action of large groups. The women in headscarves, the women in black – the chorus – are never asked for comments but are a 'voice' heard on the body, in the waiting and the weeping on the by-road of history. We often see them today behind the posing politicians in the background of TV news programmes, in newspaper photos … in community as well as domestic life. Nowhere in our Bible is their presence more significant than in Ruth's story.

The characters themselves take over a story that begins with a man of Judah and is apparently about perpetuating the memory of men who had no sons, so that in the end the book bears the genealogy but not the name of Obed. What women undertake is often written in the name of men but this story is named for Ruth, who is 'worth more than seven sons'. Ruth is clearly a book of many stories and fertile soil for poets.

Refugee

Roasted grains offered
into open hands:
water shared; bread broken
… in harmony with each other
and with God's good earth
which fed them all
in this man's
fertile land.

She had come from afar
seeking this place of refuge,
carrying her own suffering,
her hunger … and her story
deep inside her.

'Why,' she asked the good man
from Bethlehem
'are you so kind
as to notice me
a stranger in your land?'

'Come,' he said, 'I have heard
your story; you are stranger
no longer; come and eat
the fruit of my fields.
There is bread between us.'

Story in her;
story in him;
difference joyfully shared,
… pieces picked up
like broken grain
and kneaded gently
to make a new story
to change the world.

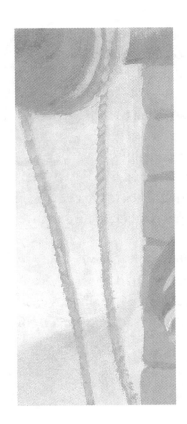

Orpah

(for all indigenous peoples)

The necessary pots and pans
weigh heavy on her back
as she travels far out
towards a country
she knows nothing about.

The story is ambivalent:
choice and no choice,
first this way
then the other way
showing the back of her neck
to Naomi and Ruth –
as if this is all
there is to tell.
She goes back to her own people
and her mother's house

to affirm self and community;
in Moabite traditions.
Here she shares memories
and the retelling of sacred stories:

her people's beginnings
in fertile valleys –
farming and fruit
and food for the feast
in Sodom and Gomorrah;
earthquakes and active volcanoes;
pillars of salt and people
named for their strength
to survive a disaster.

Orpah, princess
in her own country,
dreaming of Ruth,
Moabite stranger
in another land,
awaits images
adequate for her own telling –
knowing that everyone must live
her own beautiful story.

Women in Headscarves

Women in headscarves
watch in the background
of TV programmes and news photos.
Never quite out of sight,
their coloured heads hover
like the inconsequential flags
of a far country.
They queue with bowls or bags
waiting for bread
enough to feed a family
for this day.
Keening and singing,
mourning and dancing –
they are a presence bypassing reason,
their bodies persistent
in the flow of being;
a contemplating, forbearing
co-operating

chorus that tells another truth;
of love and mystery;
of many women imaged
in the one woman's story –
a side-road of history
yet bearing from their witness
the unforgettable name
of Ruth.

Unlike Ruth's story of hunger, Esther's is one of feasting –
everything revolves around who eats, where and with whom.
It's a story of words … and laughter.

There is something universal about the story: Esther's
resistance depends upon her knowledge of Vashti – a living
source – just as Eve depends upon knowledge of Lilith. And so
it is for most women …

Esther and Vashti

A story arranged around banquets
and who eats where
begins with Vashti
and the shades of Lilith's rebellion.

Vashti refuses to appear at a King's feast
as his showpiece, his prize,
his treasure, his darling,
and stands her ground
at the back of the palace,
laughing with the women.

Men with dented pride
issue decrees,
write to the papers,
make many speeches.
Excessive male words
attempt to ensure all women
don't follow suit
and discover for themselves
the joy of resistance.

Vashti is banished
turned out of the house
and the garden
(like Lilith … and who else?
You'll probably know …)

A virgin from unknown origins
is brought in – (why a virgin?
Think about it …)
She's handpicked from many,
prepared for a year
with oil of myrrh and other perfumes.
She's winsome and pretty
does what they expect
and feasts on no forbidden fruit
in this evocation of Eden

But when her people are threatened
and men get into difficulties
 … or are simply out drinking …
she, like many of her sisters,
reveals hidden strengths;
rises to the occasion;
sees the family fed
and the people saved.

When sweet and quiet Esther
has eaten this feast of forbidden apples,
what will she do
with her new found knowledge?

And will anyone notice her
at the back of the palace
looking for Vashti
and quietly echoing
Sarah's laughter?

*As Miriam sings and dances to celebrate freedom,
water dominates the scene: hope and life; freedom to
be carried on the bodies of the women who will
remember that water also means hardship for many
women who must carry it long miles each day. These
nameless women carry life and hope.*

Miriam's Song

Exodus 15:19–21

Miriam singing; Miriam dancing;
Miriam wonderer
walking on air.

Miriam laughing; Miriam crying;
Miriam wanderer
walking on earth.

Miriam watching; Miriam minding;
Miriam prophetess:
crafting her story.

Stepping out lightly
pulsing with beauty;
wise and far seeing,
going before us;

Trusting the dance,
willing and dreaming;
filling all lands
with the music of hope.

Women of the New Testament

Followers, messengers, lovers, friends

Blooming Women

At the garden's edge
I see the waiting women
of all time.

From the margin of history
they put the buds
of their silence
into my hands
outstretched from the future.

And the flowers that open
are vibrant and outrageous
blooming with all the colours
of a new centre of being
which is my body
and my surprise.

Followers, Messengers, Lovers, Friends

The women of the New Testament are coming out of the shadows and taking over their own story. They are followers and messengers, lovers and friends, beginning to be defined by their own standards of who they are.

Think about the uppity woman in Mark 7 (see p 85); how she understands herself – and Jesus. Then there's the woman in the sharing story (p 77) also in Mark's Gospel (12:41–44). Jesus notices her. She's a subject in her own story and her silence takes us back to that silence in Judges 19 (p 33). Perhaps the most significant of the nameless is the Samaritan woman at the well – a story in which relationship and mutuality are the water of life. It's interesting how strongly identified all these women are, even without names.

Most prophetic vision and big jumps in learning revolve around the most marginalised people in society. The storytellers show widows to be as significant in Jesus's life as they are in Elijah's. Through them Jesus values the small; through them he learns, matures, develops; through them he works out his vision of a just, related, caring society.

In one of the most famous New Testament stories – that of the wedding at Cana (John 2) – Jesus, in a down-to-earth way that recognises his mother as a whole person, addresses her as 'Woman'. He sees her as no more nor less than herself. What greater respect could he show her?

The way our Bible is arranged, this woman, Mary, is the first to enter the New Testament story. Matthew attempts to set her up as a safe and sexless example and generations since have shaped her in marble and stone and put her on a pedestal – a lifeless, passive Mary.

Luke's is a more human and down-to-earth story where solidarity between women plays an important part. Between Annunciation and Magnificat two women meet: Mary, then a barefoot country girl, yearning for life, knowing the needs and delights of ordinary people, pregnant and unmarried; Elizabeth, long unfulfilled according to Jewish culture, pregnant after her biological fertile years are over, wise and wondering – they meet and share. They hold out hands to each other in joyful companionship and commitment. These two women give us a model for relationship. They affirm each other's worth. Their words tumble out of the excitement of ordinary events. This is the kind of mutual support needed when, in response to the spirit's promptings, we set out into the unknown.

Like her ancestral sister, Hannah, Mary who sings Magnificat is defined according to her own standards. She knows that purity is more about inner attitude than outer fact; knows the possibility of transformation in all people and events; knows the sort of woman she is and the sort of child she expects. What would you expect of a child whose mother sings songs like that? Children of the Magnificat are strivers, dreamers, survivors (see p 73, 'Magnificat Now'). Magnificat is about women's voices singing not just for the sake of being heard but for the sake of a better world.

That's what this book tries to do for all the women in the stories: not only make them the subjects of their own lives – real women, watching and waiting, contemplating and co-operating, but let their voices be heard for the sake of a better world. Whether we are looking at the women waiting unseen in the garden or Mary's highly visual and senseless act of beauty with the precious oil, we see that these small incidents are big stories. They are frequently misinterpreted and misunderstood but actually grasp reality in a complex way that refuses to separate reason from feeling or spirit from body. They show, amidst rational thinking, calculating logic, continual progress, and frenzied, competitive activity, another way of thinking and being. Things aren't so very different today. Look around you. Small acts of random kindness which have huge significance happen all the time.

The sort of passivity that has so often been held up as a virtue in women is difficult to see in any of the women's stories in the Gospels! What we do see is openness to others and to the present moment in which something new is waiting to be born.

Waiting

Somewhere between Annunciation
and Magnificat;
between the angel thought
and the setting out
into the unknown
is the waiting time

when ordinary happenings:
 leaping of babies,
 conversations of home,
 holding out hands,
 in friendship and trust,
become miracles;
that bridge the gap
between loving and being.

Then the words that tumble out
of the everyday
begin to take the rhythm
of a liberation song
and the body moves wholly
towards tomorrow.

Magnificat Now

(for Bob Holman)

Luke 1

The birthing of the ordinary
revolution: women's voices
sound Magnificat
making an enormous YES

on housing estates
and travellers' sites,
in hostels for the homeless
and cardboard cities;

in community food shops,
credit unions,
soup kitchens
and baby co-ops;

where the rhythm of a song
moves the people's dreams
like flowers scattered
at the site of a stabbing;

where the handmaid
of the Lord, in her own
shaft of light
stands tall and empowered
breaking each day
in community
the 25p sliced bread
of life.

Mary's Song

Luke 1

Mary, earthy mother,
common woman:
you sing to your son
songs that will move hearts
to change the world, if only
we learn to listen
and delve to the deep
human source
of your heavenly music.

I have often wondered about the story in Matthew 2 and those men we call wise. Was it wise to ask Herod questions about a possible rival and so cause the tyrant to massacre many innocent children? Kate Compston, in her poem 'We call them wise' imagines them back at home:

I wonder if, back
in their own countries,
for all that they themselves were born again,
they heard the voice of Rachel
weeping for her children
refusing to be comforted
because they were no more?

With the shepherds, they are the only visitors to the stable that we are told about in the story. But surely others came:

Wise Women

Nobody saw them go
 – those men of the world
we fondly call wise.
They came laden with gifts
but with little to share –
kept their distance,
and left quietly
by a different route.

Back home, satisfied
that they understand
the meaning of pilgrimage

and well out of the way
of the innocents' cries,
they talk of their experiences,
feel themselves born again.

Far beyond the reach of their thinking
the morning sun touches the quiet stable
with a new day's warmth.
Women come from Bethlehem town
carrying bread freshly baked
in the star-studded night.
They come, as at every birth:
to wonder at tiny fingers and toes,
to welcome holy flesh and blood,
with the joy of touch and kiss and story,
to look deep into innocent
infant eyes, and ponder
'What will this child be?'

The women share the bread
with resurrection laughter
and moisten its earthiness
with everlasting tears –
for unnumbered nameless children die today
and the sound of Rachel's weeping
is never far away.

The man born of a woman who sung Magnificat, growing up surrounded by stories, gave his attention to people at the edge, to small things and little happenings of huge significance. In the story of the woman in the temple the focus is not so much on the smallness of the amount of the gift as on the woman herself. It's a story of a life valued, of grace and being. So much is about how we see things.

What Jesus Saw

Mark 12:41–44

Picture this:

Gold, purple, red – rich Temple colours
hold the eye – male power and status
dominate.
Controllers of the Treasury,
Leaders of the Law
parade,
give a show of prayers
for the sake of appearance.
Then make what they teach
line their own pockets;
become rich
on the backs of the poor.

Into this tableau
her head held high
comes a childless widow – the poorest
of the poor – most marginalised.

Her face is lined with suffering
but her eyes are aglow with hope
and resolution.

Powerful men stare
but cannot patronise
for here is pride and grace
in one movement –
the instant of dropping a coin
into a box and knowing herself
wholly.

The woman has treasure
beyond measure.
She is able and willing
to give; to see beyond her self
to a greater whole;
to know her value as a human being.

And watching in the shadows
of imagination
is one who looks into the heart
of all things;
who sees contrasts; makes connections;
knows about compassion and mutuality;
gives his full and loving attention
to a simple act of sharing
that has the potential
to transform a woman
and a community.

And our own insights might take the form of angels or ravens …

Watch the Ravens

1 Kings 17; Luke 7:11–17

Watch the ravens,
harbingers of doom
clothed in darkness of death
 – yet quietly feeding
resurrection hope.

Watch the ravens
carry bread to hidden prophets
waiting in the deathly wilderness.

Watch the ravens
mark the place
where death is touched,
circle the road to revelation
where a challenge to death-dealing
stops everything and compassion
for nameless sons and nameless mothers
disturbs and transforms.

Watch the ravens
as prophets put themselves
in vulnerable places alongside
the little ones of the world;

call a community
to give life to one another
to remember the Magnificat people.

Watch the ravens.
They mark the ministry of resurrection
that happens on the way
to somewhere else.

Robin Richardson and Angela Wood include this delightful tale in their book of stories and storytelling:

The Wandering Sheep

A sheep found a hole in the hedge, and scrambled through. She wandered far over the countryside and got very, very lost.

There were wild Rottweiler dogs around and they attacked and chased after the sheep. The sheep ran and ran, was utterly petrified.

The shepherd went out looking for the sheep, and found it. She fought off the dogs, and carried the sheep lovingly back to the fold.

'You must repair the hedge,' people said to the shepherd.

'No,' she said. 'I cannot fence them in. I love my sheep too much.'

It made me look again at the story of the Prodigal Son:

The Prodigal Son's Mother

Luke 15.11–32

She sits at a window
waiting in the space between
the going and the coming
remembering the runaway youth
whose whispered messages
always ended
'Don't tell Dad';
keeping a vigil
for this her own wild son –
and all turbulent children
who must run to survive.

When the fatted calf is killed
for the party, she sits apart,
and wonders
who will call the tune
when the dancing begins.

Unseen, unnamed, outside the story
she acts out her own vision
offering, amid the showy feasting,
the simple bread
of belonging and trust
– a bridge between
being and doing.

*Think about how you were first introduced to the stories from which
the following two poems came. Was it suggested then, or have you
ever heard in a sermon or Bible Study since, that the woman had a
menstrual disorder or that Jairus's daughter had reached the age of
puberty and begun menstruating? Why is the offering of food to the
girl so significant? Had she perhaps been refusing food and delay-
ing the threshold crossing into womanhood?*

Woman with Bleeding

Mark 5:30

Shalom: an end to exclusion.
Now, not he the miracle-worker
but she, daughter of the people,
is heroine in her story.

She no longer laments
blood staining her living;
lifeblood flowing from her
like children unborn.

For healing is happening
in their bodies.
The living energy of touch
liberates woman and man
to go out in wholeness:

a brave and rounded humanity
that has the right
to be called divine.

Jairus's Daughter

Mark 5:35–43

'Get up, my child!'
this is no time for sleeping.
Lighter than Lazarus,
this raising; his touch
an affirmation of womanhood
amid the misted familiar.

Flute players re-tune
to celebrate the coming
of her bleeding, and the chance
between waxing and waning
of moons, for new life.

Mother and father watch,
unable to do anything
but offer wholesome food
for the journey.
The threshold is hers
to cross alone; her knowing
is outside theirs
in the shadow of the unsaid.

Canaanite Mother

Mark 7

A Canaanite mother came to him
angry and alone; with purpose
but no necessity for meaning,
gut feeling being enough.

The child stayed behind:
a torn-apart self
in her dark world, disturbed
by unresolved relationship;
awaiting the coming of spring
and her own flowering.

There was no escaping her,
this unnamed mother
from a despised people.
She made him listen;
gave him vision
and behind her back
he gave a young life
her own balanced centre
of becoming.

Let it Happen ...

Matthew 14:13–21

What did we expect?
How did we imagine
a meal would be made?
By logic? By reason?
By economics? By market forces?

No! Women and baskets!
The surprise of the ordinary!
Thousands fed by love!
An everyday miracle
we will not allow
to happen today.

Let it happen
this most ordinary of miracles:
sharing water, bread, fish, cheese, fruit –
the contents of women's baskets
haven't changed very much.

Let it happen
the greatest miracle of all:
that people see
how things could be different,
see the hidden wisdom,
of the ones not counted.

Let it happen:
sit down with those not counted;
stop organising,
stop doing good works.
Start trusting, risking, hoping
… and sharing.
Just open your baskets
and let people be.

Martha's Faith

*Look again at Martha's confession of faith in John 12 and Peter's
in Matthew 16. Martha's confession differs from Peter's in one
poignant and beautifully significant way: she speaks of the Son of
God coming into the world.*

What world?

Not the world of angels and saints in glory;
Not the world of pulpits and church offices;
Not the world of strength and power and glory;
Not the world of kingdom but the world of community
 a world of kitchens and dirty aprons;
 of babies and nappies;
 of the daily fight against disorder and dirt;
 of the daily struggle for food, water and shelter;
 of the daily confrontation with sickness and death.

But also a world where life is given, sustained and handed on.

*With Martha we're called to believe in the resurrection here and
now; no heavenly solution; no other-worldliness; nothing exalted,
victorious, or triumphant; but full, new, growing life, which comes
out of encounter with the darkness of suffering.*

Martha

John 11:11–43

On the well travelled path
where earth stands firm
and stones slumber
mute, undisturbed, guarding
the essence of her story
she meets the one
who is always coming.

She has not taken the easy way
of passive acceptance.
She is angry:
'You are late; if you had been here
this would not have happened.'
Her misery will not destroy or drain
the energy of her crazy hope.
She brings to his coming
her own rich earthiness
absorbed from cooking bread
and feeding people
that they might live.

For he comes, her colourful Christ,
on tired, dirty feet
to a grey and ordinary place
where the stench of death
is all pervading.
But where he knows
the loosening of creative energy,
the healing touch of friends,
the rising and the freeing
of living hope.

The story in this poem which unites personal and political is powerful and its imagery often misused. Mary's act of random kindness and beauty is a gesture of love – sexual – defined by a soaring vision which is carried to a suffering world. Such visionary gestures – small, apparently insignificant, often domestic, loving and erotic – have transforming power.

Mary

John 12:1–8

At his adored and human feet
she pours out wholly and silently
the essence of her story
in sweet-scented unction
which mingles forever
with the soft womanliness
of her free flowing hair.

No cold duty to distant sovereign greatness
could initiate this act of grace.
Her body holds the fire
of luxurious, sensual loving
and her release
is moist, oily, sweet,
as it runs free for him,
and a suffering world
to which she will carry
the soaring vision
that defines her love.

Living Water

John 4:8–15

On dry, relentless paths
through stone and sand
of a thirsty land,
a man has come
to Jacob's Well,
empty-handed.
And a woman is here
clutching a jar
of precious water.
Her care is that there should be
no spill, no waste,
no dripping away.
As the man speaks
of ordinary needs
and extraordinary relationships,
an outrageous splash
of pure ecstasy
gives life
to the meeting.
Living water runs free
sweeping along hearts
grown hard as stone;
washing dusty feet
and unready hands.
This water is a precious promise
of new life
for tired people;
a flowing, moving joy,

seeking to quench human thirst
and ease everlasting sorrows.
This water is that truth
which like music or love
flows out of us
continually,
and takes us to the edge of the abyss
of faith, without the safety
of a bucket or water jar.

Wellspring

To find the well
is not what matters;
the seeking is enough.

A memory: Glendalough in the sun.
The well we do not see
opens like the womb
of mother earth;
wild, fresh water;
healing energy
flows into the river.

In such another wellspring place, a story tells,
Jesus meets the unforgettable woman
who becomes poem and dream;
a story to centre the joys
and hurts of living
in the stillness of water
 – the perfect reflection:
imagination and memory
carried on the body
beyond mind's dead ends
and mirror's distortions,
deeper than light
or thought.

I found the link between the poem 'Living Water', pinned on another woman's mirror (see p 15), and the well at Glendalough, which I didn't see but found out about from information in a guidebook left on a bench, strong enough to make another well poem.

The Last Supper

Mark 14:12–25

All day they are in the house:
Mary and Martha, Joanna and Salome,
Susannah and all the others,
baking bread,
making ready,
remembering together
other meals:
by the sea,
on the mountain,
at Emmaus …
and always hoping
there will be enough
to go round.

They move quietly
in the space
between the lines
of his story,
making a ceremonial
of love out of everyday meals.
From the beginning
they have served and shared:
memories and hopes
dreams and visions,
common friendship.

He takes the unleavened bread,
the bread of parting and haste,
the bread of our sadnesses,
passes it from man to woman,
woman to man,
from man to child,
child to woman;
from hand to hand,
lips to lips –
that with light and leavened remembering
all may feast
on immortal grain.

*(This is a timeless poem about a timeless event
– don't fall into the trap of trying to put the
chronology right!)*

Joanna, Susanna and Mary

Luke 8:1; 23:27–28, 55 and 24; 10 and 21;
Mark v 15:20; Matthew 27:55

Some women of the company
watch with the angels
from their own place –
somewhere at the margins,

where bread and wine,
spices and perfumes
loving and caring
flow freely;

where they mourn;
and cry for children
living now and
yet to be born;

where seeing
into the heart
of all things
is by the clear light
beyond death

so that the margins
are becoming a new centre.
Hopes and dreams
(men call foolish nonsense)
are leading not to chapel or church,
temple or synagogue
but to the foot of a cross:
to wonder at a story
ordinary enough to live by;
to wait silently
for men to outgrow
their madness
and the sun
to rise again.

Thoughts From the Edge ...

She has prepared food for sharing.
Friends gathered together
maybe for the last time;
her mother, comfortable just now
watching the life of the house
from her chair;
husband and children in and out;
the baby sleeping
in her cradle –
at the end
of a strangely discomforting day
– they will all eat.

The people of her day
are washed and clean.
She has wiped mouths and bums,
held young bodies tenderly
to dry them.
She has met the needs
of the mother's old body honourably
– that she may feel the beauty
of her age through her tired skin.
She has hugged and cared
and taken away dirt
with love and gentleness.

Now an unusual sense of expectancy
makes her pause for a moment
in a doorway – an in-between place
where thoughts flower –
to watch what happens
in the upper room.
She sees him take bowl and towel
to wash the feet of his friends;
sees how they hesitate, even protest;
watches the way he does it just the same

And she wonders about
hallowing the human body;
thinks how foot-washing
has mythical potential,
yet seems a pleasant task,
taking away weariness
from walking dusty roads.
Feet after all exude nothing
but salty human sweat.

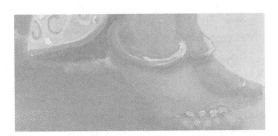

Gethsemane

At Gethsemane the skirts of light
grow wider in the immense dark,
revealing watchers at the gate. *

The women there – watching, seeing,
awake: waiting without interfering
quiet in their humble love.

While sleeping men no longer attend,
the women focus wholly
on the depths of human experience.

Helpless, baffled, marginalised,
with a precious generosity
they minister with eyes and ears.

They are waiting with patient attention
for the insight not yet given;
waiting and never relinquishing

the ability to feel; never losing
the capacity for compassion
or the strength to hope;

waiting and holding on to their vision;
forever at the gate;
forever ready.

*Legend tells that when the disciples slept in the Garden of Gethsemane
(Matthew 26:38) even though Jesus had asked them to stay awake and pray,
Mary and Martha were awake, watching and praying at the Garden gate.

The Women See ...

Mark 16

Stone is heavy with the weight
of nothing:
there at the beginning;
there when Mary comes early
to the tomb
and sees the emptiness
containing everything;

sees the morning rays
of a rising sun;
light and shadow
on each blade
of new grown grass,
fragile, transient, moving
with the weight
of eternity and endless
crucifixion.

Nothing to hold;
nothing to know.
Only the surprise
and the communion:
butterfly and bird,
her flowing tears;
love without condition
and a shout of joy.

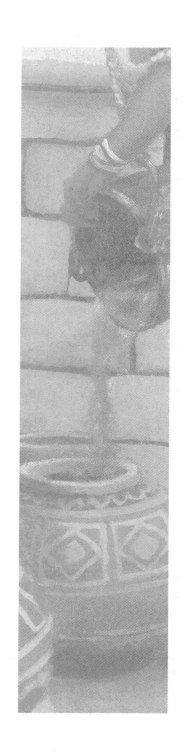

Redemption, Revelation, Resurrection ...

So this is a whole flowing story – the flow of water from Jacob's Well, the flow of Rachel's tears. *A Telling Place* is about what women do and what women say – often wordlessly. Living water is daily toil, companionship and hope. The story is about struggle – not so much against men as for recognition of alternative values. Freeing women is about more than whether they might be personally fulfilled as surgeons or accountants or priests (that battle is partly won). It is about the recognition of a whole and connected way of seeing which re-evaluates modern culture, challenges its dualistic thought patterns and reunites it with nature and its roots; it's about a perspective on society that centres on mutuality and relationship.

Women's stories and their telling reveal the interrelatedness at the heart of life: how we get on with one another; how we relate to the earth and all living things; how we see the world in which we live and into which Christ is always coming. Martha's confession of faith (see p 88) reveals that the world is relational at heart. Everything connects. I am because you are; I am because earth, air, fire, water are; I am because my parents, friends, teachers are; I am because of connections and memories ...

Informal associations of women contribute to history, personally, socially and politically. The personal becomes political when the interests of individuals and individual households are reflected in the collective actions of larger groups. Women working in solidarity make a difference. These women are all disciples. They are community people. They are, like Rachel, like the Samaritan woman, like all women at the well, sharing living water for all time.

This isn't about abstracts but about bodily experience of life. Bible women are emblematic maybe, but they are not symbols. They stand (personal) as well as stand for (political) something bigger than themselves. You can't make any of these women into symbols alone. They take over their own lives. They insist on being real, not because they existed (whether any of them did or not doesn't matter) but because their stories are our own; their voices and silences help us to interpret and live our own stories – and that is revelation.

I hope this book has been her-story: incarnational theology rooted in Martha's Confession of Faith; earthed in creation and the possibility of transformation – and that is redemption.

Life goes on, as Sarah, Rachel, Esther, Ruth, Mary, Martha and all the others knew … in tears, in love and in laughter freed for ever and ever – and that is resurrection.

In the margins of books
shadows of unknowing
pattern the pages.
Pencil ponderings
underline, make quiet
announcements – a word here
a paragraph there.
Insights search
for images.

Cherished connections
are gently made
from the marks
of our human-ness:
finger prints;
a smudge of blood;
the stain of a tear.
Another story
rests in these interruptions …

like Hagar in the wilderness
waiting;
Miriam by the sea
dancing;
Mary in the stable
wondering –
after the visitors leave.

Back in the ordinary place
somewhere in the margins
of history –
in the kitchen, maybe –
annunciation is always
happening.

References

Quote on page 23 from 'Lilith's Dance', a poem by Michelene Wandor from *Gardens of Eden Revisited*, Five Leaves, Nottingham 1999.

Page 27: Judith Plaskow's commentary on which this story of Lilith and Eve is based appears in *Womanguides*, Rosemary Radford Reuther, Beacon Press, p.19.

Quote on page 75 from the poem 'We call them wise' by Kate Compston, from *Celebrating Women*, SPCK, London, 1995, p39.

Quote on page 81 from *Inside Stories*, by Angela Wood and Robin Richardson, Trentham Books Ltd (Westview House, 734 London Road, Oakhill, Stoke-on-Trent, Staffs SYT4 5NP),1992, p.50.

Acknowledgements are also due to the editors of the following publications in which some of the poems originally appeared:

Connect (at one time the national magazine of the Methodist Church); *The Epworth Review*; *Celebrating Women* (SPCK); and *Dandelions and Thistles* and *Dreaming of Eden* (Wild Goose Publications).

Thanks

Many friends encouraged this book into being and I am grateful to them all. I would like especially to thank Jan Sutch Pickard and Fred and Anthea Kaan for their unfailing friendship, support and generosity. Thank you also to Sandra Kramer and all at Wild Goose Publications. Working with them is a privilege and a joy.

The Iona Community

The Iona Community, founded in 1938 by the Revd George MacLeod, then a parish minister in Glasgow, is an ecumenical Christian community committed to seeking new ways of living the Gospel in today's world. Initially working to restore part of the medieval abbey on Iona, the Community today remains committed to 'rebuilding the common life' through working for social and political change, striving for the renewal of the church with an ecumenical emphasis, and exploring new, more inclusive approaches to worship, all based on an integrated understanding of spirituality.

The Community now has over 240 Members, about 1500 Associate Members and around 1500 Friends. The Members – women and men from many denominations and backgrounds (lay and ordained), living throughout Britain with a few overseas – are committed to a fivefold Rule of devotional discipline, sharing and accounting for use of time and money, regular meeting, and action for justice and peace.

At the Community's three residential centres – the Abbey and the MacLeod Centre on Iona, and Camas Adventure Camp on the Ross of Mull – guests are welcomed from March to October and over Christmas. Hospitality is provided for over 110 people, along with a unique opportunity, usually through week-long programmes, to extend horizons and forge relationships through sharing an experience of the common life in worship, work, discussion and relaxation. The Community's shop on Iona, just outside the Abbey grounds, carries an attractive range of books and craft goods.

The Community's administrative headquarters are in Glasgow, which also serves as a base for its work with young people, the Wild Goose Resource Group working in the field of worship, a bi-monthly magazine, *Coracle*, and a publishing house, Wild Goose Publications.

For information on the Iona Community contact:
The Iona Community, Fourth Floor, Savoy House,
140 Sauchiehall Street, Glasgow G2 3DH, UK
Phone: +44 (0)141 332 6343
e-mail: ionacomm@gla.iona.org.uk web: www.iona.org.uk

For enquiries about visiting Iona, please contact:
Iona Abbey, Isle of Iona, Argyll PA76 6SN, UK
Phone: +44 (0)1681 700404 e-mail: ionacomm@iona.org.uk

More Books from Wild Goose

THE ONE LOAF
An everyday celebration
Joy Mead

A book which explores the making and the mystery of bread –
growing, making, baking, sharing – in story and recipe, poetry
and prayer. In bread we see the true connectedness of all life –
the uniting of body and soul, spirit and material. It is not just a
symbol of life, it is life itself. Without food, life is impossible, so
eating becomes sacred. Take and eat means take and live; to
share food is to share our life. Jesus, in a simple act, made eating
and sharing sacred. This beautiful illustrated book helps us to
love the 'dailiness' of bread, the holiness of eating and the justice
of sharing.

160pp. · 1 901557 38 3 · £10.99

DANDELIONS AND THISTLES
Biblical meditations from the Iona Community
Jan Sutch Pickard (ed)

A beautiful, illustrated book presenting Bible stories in the
form of radical, thought-provoking meditations by various
contributors. These monologues, scripts and poems give
profound and sensitive messages in a simple and direct style
accessible to all, making them perfect for use in group or
worship situations or for individual reflection.

Contributors include: Jan Sutch Pickard · Kate McIlhagga ·
John L. Bell · Joy Mead · Ruth Burgess · Yvonne Morland ·
David Osborne · Kathy Galloway · Norman Shanks · John
Davies · Anna Briggs

1999 · 96pp · 1 901557 14 6 · £9.99

Wild Goose Publications, the publishing house of the Iona Community established in the Celtic Christian tradition of St Columba, produces books, tapes and CDs on:

- holistic spirituality
- social justice
- political and peace issues
- healing
- innovative approaches to worship
- song in worship, including the work of the Wild Goose Resource Group
- material for meditation and reflection

If you would like to find out more about our books, tapes and CDs, contact us at:

Wild Goose Publications
Fourth Floor, Savoy House
140 Sauchiehall Street,
Glasgow G2 3DH, UK

Tel. +44 (0)141 332 6292
Fax +44 (0)141 332 1090
e-mail: admin@ionabooks.com

or visit our website at
www.ionabooks.com
for details of all our products and online sales